# MACBOOK PRO 2020

## A Simplified Step By Step Guide On How To Use The New MacBook Pro 2020 With Examples, Tricks, Tips and shortcut.

### BY

### Kasper Frederik Hansen

**Table of Contents**

# CHAPTER ONE

# APPLE MACBOOK PRO 13 (2020) REVIEW

**Review of the Apple MacBook Pro 13**

The keyboard that is on the new MacBook Pro gives it a reliable choice for aspiring creators.

An industry-leading display

Slim and lightweight design

Excellent new keyboard

Solid build quality

Wizard options are tantalizing

Average battery life

MacBook Pro 13 plays an important role in Apple's lineup. Not a true "pro" laptop, it's the MacBook Pro 16. It's for the hobbyist. amateur. Ambitious professional.

Let's be honest. The real number of persons who really require professional performance is small, while amateur graphic designers, YouTubers, music producers, and photographers are a dime a dozen.

## Price and configurations

Apple's pricing method for the MacBook Pro reflects the precipitous nature of this laptop. It's too expensive. Even more expensive than before. The base model starts at $ 1,299, which seems like a fair price.

This is until you realize that Apple is selling old hardware on a new laptop. Keyboard aside, this "new" MacBook Pro is identical to what was sold a year ago.

This is not what other laptop manufacturers do. You can get the latest 10th generation processors on the Dell XPS 13, Surface Laptop 3, or HP Specter x360 in configurations starting at $ 1,200 or less. This is not a standard Apple practice either. The company tends to update its Macs at a slower rate than other companies, but when a new model appears, it often contains the latest silicone.

And I can't imagine Apple releasing a flagship new iPhone or iPad using a processor last year. Instead, it launches older designs with new processors, like the iPhone SE.

This makes the MacBook Pro setup a complete disaster. Good luck in selecting between the 8th Gen Core i7 versus the 10th Gen Core i5. Interestingly, the eighth generation costs $ 100 more when configured similarly. Specifications versus specs, Apple charges you $ 200 for the modest jump from 8th to 10th generation Intel processors. It also charges more for faster memory, possibly in an effort to improve the deal on high-end models.

There is a ray of light in the new settings. storage. The base model now comes with a 256GB SSD instead of 128GB, and the $ 1799 model has 512GB. This is already the standard for many laptops, and I'm glad to see Apple doing the same.

## performance

One thing that could change my bitter impression of the MacBook Pro 13's options.

**Performance.** Apple may have brought something special. This is possible because the 10th generation Intel

Core chipset in the most expensive configurations is for the MacBook Pro.

My review unit had an Intel Core i5-1038NG7 processor, which is a 25W 4-core and eight threaded processors. It's similar to the Intel Core i5-1035G7 processor, which is a 15W processor that appears in many 13-inch laptops, including the Dell XPS 13, HP Specter x360, and Microsoft Surface Laptop3.

The extra 10 watts add some performance, but as you may have learned, it's a modest increase. The MacBook Pro 13 beats most of the other 13-inch laptops in the Cinebench R20 and Geekbench 5, especially laptops that don't put too much CPU stress, like the Specter x360 or the Razer Blade Stealth. The Dell XPS 13 is also a good example. It uses thermal tricks to boost the processor the most, and despite having a low-power chip, it beats the MacBook Pro 13 in most benchmarks.

Again, that's with the $ 1,799 model, with a 10th-gen Core i5 processor, 16GB of RAM, and 512GB of storage.

That doesn't justify the fact that MacBook Pro is a content creation machine. Exporting a 4K 2-minute clip to ProRes

422 took 16 minutes painfully long. The problem is, the laptop starts at $ 2,499, more than twice the price.

# CHAPTER TWO

# HOW TO SET YOUR MacBook

The first time you start your MacBook Pro, the Setup Assistant guides you through the easy steps to get started with your new Mac. If you want to transfer your data from another computer, see Transfer your data to your new MacBook Pro to get more details.

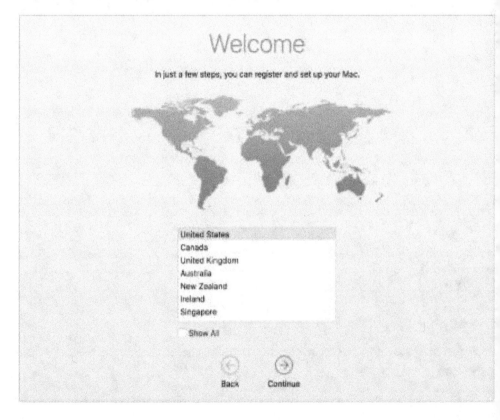

The Mac screen with Setup Wizard displays the Welcome screen.

Make sure you're connected to Wi-Fi, turn on Bluetooth® wireless technology, get an Apple ID, then sign in to your device. Activate Siri during setup, if desired. You can also activate Touch ID and Apple Pay on the device.

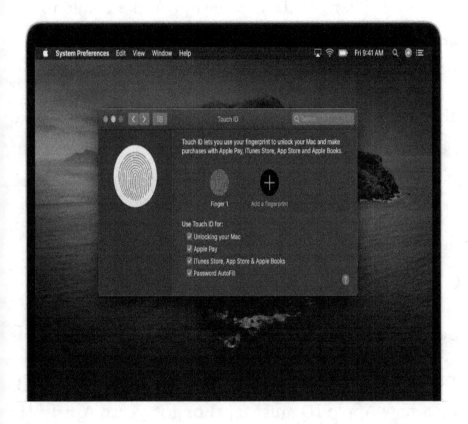

Sign in with your Apple ID. Your Apple ID is the account you use for everything you do with Apple, including using the App Store, iTunes Store, iCloud, Messages, and more.

Your Apple ID will include an email address and a unique password. You only need an Apple ID to use any Apple service, on any device, whether it's a computer, an iOS device, an iPad, or an Apple Watch. It is better if you have your own Apple ID and don't share it.

If you don't have an Apple ID yet, you can create one during setup (it's free). To create your Apple ID, go to the Apple ID account website, and create an Apple ID for yourself.

If other family members are using Apple devices, make sure each family member has their own Apple ID. You can create Apple ID accounts for your children and share purchases and subscriptions with Family Sharing. See Apple Account on Mac.

**Important:**

 If you forgot your Apple ID password, you do not need to create a new Apple ID. Just tap **Forgot your Apple ID and password?** in the login, window to retrieve and get back your password.

You can quickly and easily carry out setup tasks with the setup wizard, but if you want to do them later, follow these steps:

Choose a light or dark look. If you wish to change the option you choose when setting up your Mac, tap on the System Preferences icon in the Dock, or choose Apple menu> System Preferences. Click General, then select Light, Dark, or Automatic for your theme. You can also choose other appearance that you prefer here also.

**Connect to a Wi-Fi network**

. Click the Wi-Fi status icon in the menu bar, then choose your Wi-Fi network and enter the password, if needed.

**Turn Wi-Fi on or off**

. Click on the Wi-Fi icon in the menu bar, and select Turn Wi-Fi On or Turn Wi-Fi Off.

**Turn Bluetooth on or off.**

Tap on the Bluetooth icon in the menu bar, and select Turn Bluetooth On or Turn Bluetooth Off.

## Set up iCloud on your MacBook Pro

With the help of iCloud, you can store all of your content - documents, movies, music, photos, and more - in the cloud and access it from anywhere.

## To configure iCloud

choose Apple menu> System Preferences. Log in with your Apple Login ID. Click Apple ID iCloud, then choose the features you want to use. For more information, see Access your iCloud content on your Mac.

## Important:

Make sure you sign in with the same Apple ID on your device

**Set up 'Hey Siri'.** On MacBook Pro, you can simply say "**Hey Siri**" to receive responses to your requests. To enable this feature in the Siri System Preferences panel, click "Listen" **Hey Siri,** "then say the various Siri commands when prompted.

## Set up Touch ID

You can add a fingerprint to Touch ID when you want to set up. For you to set up Touch ID, Click the System Preferences in the Dock, Then tap Touch ID. To add a fingerprint, click the "Add" button and follow the on-screen instructions.

## Touch ID

 preferences window with options to add a fingerprint, use Touch ID to unlock your Mac, use Apple Pay, and make purchases from the iTunes Store, App Store, and Book Store.

You can also configure options for how you want to use Touch ID on a MacBook Pro:

Unlock your Mac instead of inputting your password

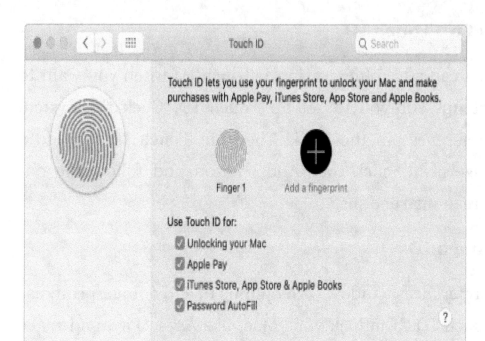

Touch ID lets you use your fingerprint to unlock your Mac and make purchases with Apple Pay, iTunes Store, App Store and Apple Books.

Finger 1   Add a fingerprint

Use Touch ID for:

☑ Unlocking your Mac
☑ Apple Pay
☑ iTunes Store, App Store & Apple Books
☑ Password AutoFill

# CHAPTER THREE

# STEPS ON HOW TO LOCATE AND FIND THE APPLICATIONS FOLDER ON YOUR MACBOOK PRO DEVICE AND PIN APPS TO YOUR DOCK

You can find the Apps folder easily on your Macbook pro device using the Finder tool.

You can also add the apps you use often to the Dock to make it easier to access.

**How to find Apps on your Macbook pro.**

Here's what to do to access the Applications folder and how to optimize the Dock at the bottom of the screen to easily access the apps you use the most.

# Here is how to find Apps folder on your Macbook pro

The Applications folder contains all those applications that make your computer a valuable tool. Here's how to find it quickly and easily on your Mac.

1. Click the "Finder" application, it looks like a blue and white face and is in the Dock.

Is your Finder is hidden in the Dock? Click on any empty space on the desktop to set Finder as the current application in the menu bar in the upper-left corner of your screen. Then Tap on File and choose the New Finder Window.

2. Select "Applications" in the left sidebar.

## How to add apps to your Dock

1. Open the app whose base you want to keep, it will appear to the right of the apps already installed in its base.

2. Right-click on the application icon in the Dock and select "Options" then "Keep in Dock".

# CHAPTER FOUR

# KNOW ABOUT MACBOOK PRO KEYBOARDS AND SHORTCUTS

By using certain keys on the keyboard, you can do things that would normally require a mouse, trackpad, or other input devices.

For you to be able to use a keyboard shortcut, press and hold one or more keys, and then press the last shortcut key. For instance, let us say, to use Command-C to copy, press, and hold the Command key, and then the C key, and then release both keys. Mac keyboards and menus often use symbols for specific keys, including modifier keys:

Touch ID

## keys:

Command (or cmd)

Shift ⇧

Option (or alternative) ⌥

Control (or Ctrl) ^

Caps Lock ⇪

## The National Front

Some keys on some Apple keyboards contain special functions and symbols, such as screen brightness, keyboard brightness, task control, and more. If these functions are not available on your keyboard, you can reproduce some of them by creating your own keyboard shortcuts. To use these function keys as F1, F2, F3, or other keys, combine them with the Fn key.

Cut, copy, paste and other common shortcuts

**Command-X**: Cut the selected item and temporarily store it on the clipboard.

**Command-C:** Copy marked items to the clipboard on your MacBook pro.

**Command-V**: Paste the contents of the clipboard into the current document or application.

**Command-Z:** Undo the previous command. You can then press Shift-**Command-Z** to redo and invert the Undo command. In some applications, you can undo and return different commands.

**Command-A**: Select all items.

**Command-F**: Search for items in a document or open a search window.

**Command-G:** Find Again - Find the next occurrence of the previously found element. To find the previous duplicate, press Shift-Command-G.

**Command-H**: Hide front app windows. To see the front app and hide all other apps, press the Option key, Command, and H.

**Command-M**: Minimize the front window to the Dock. To minimize all of the app's front windows, press Option-Command-M.

**Command-O**: Opens the selected item or opens a dialog to select a file to open.

**Command-P**: Print the current document.

**Command-S**: Save the current document.

**Command-T**: Open a new tab.

**Command-W**: Close the front window. To close all application windows, press Option-Command-W.

**Option-Command-Esc**: Force an application to close.

**Command AND Spacebar**: to display or hide the Spotlight search area. To perform a Spotlight search from the Finder window, press Command - **Option - Spacebar. Control - Command - Space bar**: Displays a character viewer, with which you can choose emoji and other symbols.

**Control-Command-F**: Use the app in full-screen mode, if the app supports it.

**Spacebar**: Use Quick View to preview the selected item.

**Command-Tab:** Switch to the last used app between open apps.

**Shift-Command-5**: On macOS Mojave or later, take a screenshot or record a screen. Or use Shift-Command-3 or Shift-Command-4 to get screenshots.

**Shift-Command-N**: Create a new folder in Finder.

**Command-Comma** (,): Open the preferences for the front application.

Sleep, log out and close shortcuts

You may need to press and hold some of these shortcuts a little longer than others. This helps you avoid unintended use.

**Power button** - Press to turn on or wake your Mac. Press and make sure you hold it for 1.5 seconds to put your Macbook pro to sleep. * Keep pressing to force your Mac to shut down.

**Control - Shift - Power Button * or Control - Shift - Media Eject**: Put your screens to sleep.

**Control - Power Button * or Control - Media Eject** - displays a dialog asking if you want to restart, suspend, or stop playback.

**Control - Command - Power Button: *** Force your Mac to restart, without prompting you to save open and unsaved documents.

**Control - Command - Eject Media**: Close all applications then restart your Mac. If any open documents have unsaved changes, you will be asked if you want to save them.

# CHAPTER FIVE

# WHAT YOU CAN SEE ON THE MENU BAR ON YOUR MACBOOK PRO

The menu bar can be located exactly at the top of the Mac screen. The menu bar. On the left side of the device is the Apple menu and other apps menus. To the right are the Status menus, Spotlight, Siri, and Notification Center icons.

You can configure an option in the general preferences to hide the menu bar automatically; Then it is only displayed when you move the cursor to the top of the screen.

## Apple menu

**The Apple menu**, This can be located on the upper-left corner of your screen, it contains commands for things you do frequently, like update apps, open system preferences, lock the screen, or turn off your Mac.

## Application lists

The application menus are located next to the Apple menu. The name of the application you're using appears in bold, followed by other menus, often with standard names like File, Edit, Format, or Window. Each app has a help menu to make it easy to get information about using the app.

**Status Lists**

To the far right of the menu bar are the status menus, and they are usually represented by icons. Use these lists to check the condition of your Mac or quickly access features; For example, quickly turn Wi-Fi on or off or check your computer's battery charge.

**Status Lists.**

You can add status menus, such as the emoji viewer or the volume control icon. You can also add status lists to some apps when installed.

To rearrange the status menu icons, press and hold the Command key while you drag the items. To delete an icon, hold down the Command key and drag the icon out of the menu bar.

## Highlight

Click the Spotlight icon, present after the Status Menus, to use Spotlight to find items on your Mac and more.

## Siri

After Spotlight is the Siri icon - click on it to ask Siri to do things like open files or apps, or search for things on your Mac or the Internet. You can easily have Siri results at your fingertips on the desktop or in the notification center.

## Notification Center

On the far right of the menu bar, click the Notification Center icon to use Notification Center to view the details of your day and track notifications that you missed.

# CHAPTER SIX

# HOW TO USE THE DOCK ON MAC

The Dock on the Macbook pro desktop is a reliable place to access apps and other features that you probably use every day. The Dock can display up to three recently used applications that are not yet in the Dock and a folder for items you download from the Internet.

The Dock displays the icons for the application, download stack, and container.

Open items in the Dock

**On your Mac's Dock, do one of the following**:

Open an app: Click the app icon. For instance, if you want to open the Finder, click the Finder icon in the Dock.

Open a file in the application: drag the file over the application icon. For example, to open a document that you created in Pages, drag the document over the Pages icon in the Dock.

**To show an item in the Finder**: Command + tap on the item's icon.

Switch to the previous application and hide the current application: Option-click the icon of the current application.

Switch to another application and hide all others: Option-click and command the icon of the application you want to switch to.

You can press Control and click an item to display a shortcut menu of other actions to perform, such as opening or closing an application, opening a recent document, and more.

If an application stops responding, you can force close the application from the Dock (you may lose unsaved changes). Control-Option-click the application icon, then select Force Quit.

Add or remove items from the Dock

**On your Mac, do the following**:

**Input an item to the Dock**: move the apps to the left side of the line that divides recently used apps. Drag files and folders to the right side of the other line that separates recently used applications. An alias is placed for the item in the Dock.

**Delete an item from the Dock**: Drag the item out of the Dock until you see Delete.

**Note:**

Only the alias will be removed; The real item will remain on your Macbook pro device.

If you accidentally delete an app's icon from the Dock, it's easy to put it back (the app is still on your Mac). Open the application so that its icon reappears in the Dock. Hold down the Control key and click the app icon, then choose Options> Keep in Dock.

You can also rearrange items in the Dock if you would like to just drag an item to a new location on your MacBook pro.

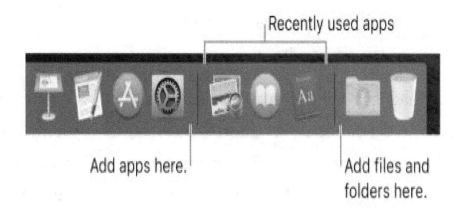

Recently used apps

Add apps here.

Add files and folders here.

## Customize the dock

On your Mac, choose Apple menu> System Preferences and then click on the Dock.

Change the options you want.

For example, you can change how items appear in the Dock, adjust their size and position, or even hide them.

To see the options, click the Help button in the section.

To quickly change the size or resize the Dock, place the pointer over the dividing line until a double arrow appears, then drag the Dock to make it larger or smaller.

You can use keyboard shortcuts to move to the Dock. Press Control-F3 to go to the Dock. Then use the left and right arrow keys to move from one symbol to another. Click Back to open an item.

A red badge on an icon in the Dock indicates that you must perform one or more actions in System or Application Preferences. For example, the red badge on the Mail icon in the Dock indicates that you have new email messages to read.

When you drag a folder to the Dock, it can display it as a stack of folders. ordinarily, the Dock in your Mac also comes with the Downloads package. See Organize files in stacks.

# CHAPTER SEVEN

# GUIDELINES ON HOW TO USE THE TOUCH BAR ON YOUR NEW MACBOOK PRO DEVICE

The Touch Bar on MacBook Pro gives you quick access to commands on your Mac, and it changes automatically based on what you do and the applications you use. The Touch Bar is available in 2016 or later MacBook Pro models, except for MacBook Pro (13-inch, 2016, 2 Thunderbolt 3) and MacBook Pro (13-inch, 2017, 2 Thunderbolt 3).

**Find controls and system settings on the control strip**

When you start up the MacBook Pro, the control strip on the right side of the Touch Bar shows some familiar buttons like Volume, Mute, and Screen Brightness, in addition to Siri. Press the Expand button on the Control Strip to access controls such as Brightness, Mission Control, Launchpad, and Media Playback.

16-inch MacBook Pro with Touch Bar

To access the function buttons F1 - F12 on the touch bar, press the function button (fn) at the bottom left of the keyboard.

The 16-inch MacBook Pro with Touch Bar has a dedicated Escape (Esc) key. The 13-inch or 15-inch MacBook Pro, the Touch Bar, the Escape button appears on the left side of the Touch Bar.

Explore the touch bar in apps

Many of the applications built into the Mac have touch bar controls that make common actions easy. For example, in Mail, you can use the Touch Bar to create, reply to, archive, and mark messages as junk.

When you select the text, the Touch Bar displays formatting options such as bold, italic, and menus.

**Customize the touch bar**

In many applications, such as Finder, Mail, and Safari, you can customize the Touch Bar.

Choose View> Personalize Touch Bar. The Personalization window appears on your screen, allowing you to choose your favorite items:

When you customize the Touch Bar, its buttons vibrate. Use the cursor to drag the items you want from the screen onto the touch bar.

**Customize the control bar**

You can also add, remove, or rearrange buttons on the control strip, including **Siri**.

In any application that supports customization (such as Finder), select View> Customize Touch Bar. Tap the

Control Strip area on the Touch Bar to switch to Control Strip customization.

Then use the cursor to drag the items you want from the screen to the control bar.

Also, you can enter Control Strip customization mode by tapping **the Custom Control Strip** on the Keyboard section of System Preferences.

## Use accessibility options with the touch bar

Accessibility features that help you use your Macbook Pro can also assist you to use the Touch Bar. Hold down the Command key while pressing the Touch ID (power button) three times to toggle VoiceOver, which reads the Touch Bar commands out loud. high.

# CHAPTER EIGHT

## GUIDLINES ON HOW TO USE THE TOUCH BAR ON YOUR NEW MACBOOK PRO

When Apple updated the MacBook Pro in 2016, among its list of updates and new features was the so-called Touch Bar, which is a slim touch screen that sits on the top of the keyboard instead of the functions keys. The company has since released updated MacBook Pro models for 2017 (we cover it here: 2017 15-inch MacBook Pro review and 2017 13-inch MacBook Pro review), and these have the upper hand.

We will show you how to use the Touch Bar on these MacBook Pro models - including how to change its functionality for various commonly used applications, and how to customize the Touch Bar to display and perform exactly the functions you want.

**What Macs have Touch Bar?**

The Touch Bar is only available on select 2016 and 2017 15-inch and 13-inch MacBook Pro models.

**These include current 2017 models:**

13-inch 'Kaby Lake' processor, 7th generation 3.1GHz dual-core, 256GB storage, £ 1749

Kaby Lake dual-core 13-inch 3.GHz to 3.GHz processor, 512GB storage, £ 1949

15-inch 'Kaby Lake' quad-core processor clocked at 2.8GHz, 256GB of storage, £ 2,349

15-inch 2.9GHz quad-core 'Kaby Lake' processor, 512GB storage, £ 2,699

**And these 2016 models, which you can find second-hand or in a revamped Apple store**

Skylake 6th Gen 13in Dual-Core 2.9GHz, 256GB Storage, was £ 1,749

Skylake sixth-generation 13-inch, 2.9GHz dual-core, 512GB of storage, was £ 1949

Skylake sixth-gen 15-inch 2.6GHz quad-core 256GB storage, was £ 2,349

Skylake 6th-gen 15-inch 2.7GHz quad-core processor, 512GB of storage, £ 2,699

Read Next: Mac Buying Guide 2017 | Best cheap MacBook Pro deals in the UK

# CHAPTER NINE

# STEPS TO USE THE TOUCH BAR ON THE NEW MACBOOK PRO 2020

**Touch Bar Tips**

There are a number of ways that the Touch Bar can simplify the tasks you frequently do on a Mac. One of our favorites is the ease with which we can correct spelling mistakes, simply by clicking on the correct word.

**Guidelines on how to use the touch bar to unlock your Mac**

If you have set up a MacBook Pro with the Touch Bar, you must add your fingerprint which can be used as a form of identification to unlock a Mac or to confirm your identity for iTunes purchases or for use with Apple Pay.

You can also add fingerprints later by going to System Preferences> Touch ID

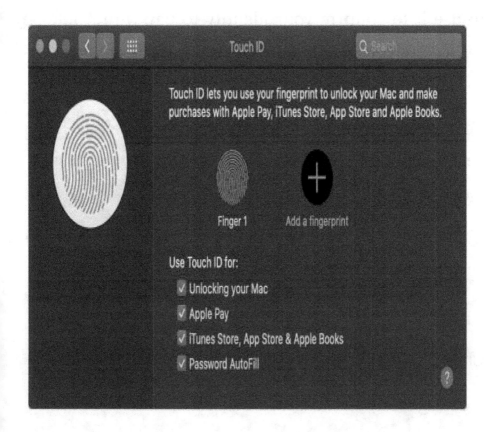

Select Add a fingerprint and tap the small square area next to the touch bar while the built-in camera captures your fingerprint

Now when you unlock your Mac, you don't need to enter your password, just place your finger on the Touch ID panel

If you set Fingerprint to use it to unlock your Mac, according to the instructions above, you will also be able to use it to confirm your identity to pay with Apple Pay, for example when buying something from the Apple web store.

You will need to update your Apple Pay preferences and verify your Mac with your bank before you can use it to pay with Apple Pay.

## guidelines to customize the control strip on the touch bar on the MacBook pro

Open System Preferences> Keyboard

Click Customize Control Bar

Existing icons on the Touch Bar will vibrate

Drag and drop new icons onto the touch bar, like Spotlight Search

Adding Favorite Apps to Touch Bar

I wish we could add your favorite apps to the touch bar, or make the touch bar mirror the dock, but that's not possible yet.

## How to adjust the brightness using the touch bar

There are tons of Touch Bar options available at all times, Apple calls them the **Control Strip** - brightness is one of them

If you click on the icon that looks like the sun, a slider will appear on the touch bar, touch, and move your finger until the screen brightness the one you want.

## How to adjust the volume using the touch bar

There is a shortcut for the volume controls also in the Control Strip section of the Touch Bar

Tap the icon that has a speaker shape

Use the slider bar on your MacBook pro to increase or decrease the volume to your specification

To mute the volume, simply tap the icon that shows a speaker line by line

## steps to open Siri using the touch bar on your device

One of the best things about the Touch Bar is the presence of the Siri button (something we wish was present on all Apple keyboards).

Click the Siri icon, the circle with a wave-like form.

# CHAPTER TEN

# STEPS ON HOW TO MAKE EVERYTHING BIGGER ON MY DEVICE SCREEN

Do you have trouble reading things on your laptop? Do you want to enlarge everything on your screen?

On a Mac, the easiest way to enlarge everything on the screen is to lower the screen resolution.

**Steps:**

First, click on the Apple menu at the top left of the screen and select System Preferences. Click the Displays icon, and then make sure the Display tab is highlighted. From there, look for the Resolution poster. If so, click "Scale". Next, a list of five options will appear. The option on the left will produce the most text, while the option on the right will produce the smallest text (and will increase the total screen space available).

On older Macs, there will be a Screen Resolution menu on the left side of the window. The smaller the number, the bigger everything will appear. Try different numbers until you find the right setting for you.

# CHAPTER ELEVEN

## STEPS TO CUT, COPY, AND PASTE FILES ON YOUR MACBOOK PRO

The style used by Macbook pro devices may seem like it to new users, but OS X allows copy, paste, and cut.

### Use the command key

There are two ways to copy and paste items on your MacBook Pro, first by selecting the file and holding Command + C to copy, then Command + V to paste the item where you want the copied item to be.

### Use the option key

The second is faster and less known: with the mouse and the Option key. The default behavior of the system generally moves the file dragged with the mouse (basically cut and paste), but holding down the Option key will make a copy of the file, just as if you had used the copy/paste functions in any normal application.

### Hold down the command and drag

However, there is a situation where the default behavior of dragging the mouse is reversed. OS X will try to copy files that are dragged between drives, such as in a network enclosure. For those cases, you can hold down the Command key while reviewing the file. You will notice that the "plus" symbol will disappear, which means that it is not copied, but is clipped. The file will be transferred from the drive it is on to the new drive, leaving no copy on both drives. Unfortunately, the keyboard shortcut for Cut (Command + X) does not work for files.

# CHAPTER TWELVE

# STEPS TO TAKE IF MAIL ON YOUR MACBOOK PRO 2020 ALWAYS ASK FOR PASSWORD

**Why is the publication asking for your password?**

Mail asks for your password when it communicates with your email provider, but it cannot contact your email account because your email provider does not accept your email password.

**Mail connection error**

The email provider may deny your password for various reasons, including:

You are not using your current email password. If you updated the password on another device, make sure you are using the same password on your Mac.

Your email provider has deactivated or suspended your account. Contact your email provider for assistance.

## Verify your password in Internet Accounts preferences

You may be able to correct your password as follows, this may depend on the type of email account you have and you are using on your device:

Get out of the mail. If he doesn't withdraw, you can force him to do so.

Choose Apple menu > System Preferences, and then click Internet Accounts.

Select your email account in the sidebar.

If you see the password field for your account, remove the password and enter the correct password.

Cancel System Preferences, and open Email and use your account again.

If Mail keeps asking for your password, the password may be wrong. Your mail provider can assist you to verify your email settings and ensure that you are using the correct password on your device.

## Try webmail

Many email service providers offer webmail, which is a way to use an email with a web browser like Safari, rather than using an email application like Mail. For example, if you use an iCloud email account, you can use iCloud.com to send and receive an email.

## Delete your account, then add it again

If no other solution worked, try setting up your email account again. To do this, first, delete your email account and then add the account again.

If you use Apple iCloud Mail, learn how to troubleshoot problems with iCloud Mail. Find out what to do if you forgot your Apple ID password or want to change your Apple ID password.

# CHAPTER THIRTEEN

# STEPS ON HOW TO CONNECT TO THE INTERNET WITH YOUR MACBOOK PRO DEVICE

Learn to use Wi-Fi, Personal Hotspot, and Ethernet to connect to the Internet.

## Connect to a Wi-Fi network

Select the Wi-Fi icon on the menu bar on the device, then choose a network. If the Wi-Fi connection is inactive, tap the Wi-Fi off icon, and then select Turn Wi-Fi on.

If you are connecting your device to a public Wi-Fi network, a window may pop-up with terms and conditions that you will accept before you can connect.

## Connect to a secure Wi-Fi network

Secure Wi-Fi networks are password-protected and have a lock code in their name.

select the Wi-Fi icon on the menu bar of your device. If the Wi-Fi connection is inactive, tap the Wi-Fi off icon, and then choose Turn Wi-Fi on. *

**Network selection**.

Enter the password, then click "Join". If you do not know the Wi-Fi password, contact your network administrator.

### Connect to a hidden network

Select the Wi-Fi icon on the menu bar in your device. If Wi-Fi is off, choose the Wi-Fi off icon, then choose Turn Wi-Fi on. *

**Choose to join another network**.

Enter the name of the network. Make sure you have entered the correct network name.

If the network is secure, choose the type of security and then enter the password.

Click Join.

### Create a Wi-Fi network

If you have Internet service at your location, you can connect a third-party AirPort base station or router to your modem to create a Wi-Fi network. Use the setup guide for your AirPort base station or refer to your third-party router's guide for help.

* If you don't see the Wi-Fi icon in the menu bar, you can add it again. Go to Apple menu select System Preferences,and select Network, click on Wi-Fi, and then choose "Show Wi-Fi status in the menu bar."

## Use a personal access point

With most carrier plans, you can share your iPhone or iPad's mobile data connection (Wi-Fi + Cellular) with your Mac.

## Learn to configure Personal Hotspot.

## Using Ethernet

To connect to the Internet through a wired connection, connect an Ethernet cable between the router or modem and the Ethernet icon on the Ethernet port on the Mac.

Some Macs require an Ethernet adapter such as the Belkin USB-C to Gigabit Ethernet Adapter or the Apple Thunderbolt to Gigabit Ethernet Adapter.

* If you don't see the Wi-Fi icon in the menu bar, you can add it again. select the Apple menu, Tap System Preferences, select Network, select Wi-Fi, and then choose "Show Wi-Fi status in the menu bar."

## Use a personal access point

With most carrier plans, you can share your iPhone or iPad's mobile data connection (Wi-Fi + Cellular) with your Mac.

## Using Ethernet

To connect to the Internet through a wired connection, connect an Ethernet cable between the router or modem and the Ethernet icon on the Ethernet port on the Mac.

# CHAPTER FIFTEEN

# USE MULTI-TOUCH GESTURES ON YOUR MAC

With the multi-touch control panel or the magic mouse, you can click, slide, tap, or extend one or more fingers to perform useful actions.

**Touchpad gestures**.

Trackpad gestures require a built-in Magic Trackpad or Multi-Touch trackpad. If your trackpad supports Force Touch, you can also play hard and get haptic feedback.

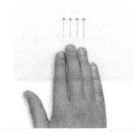

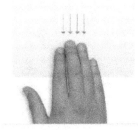

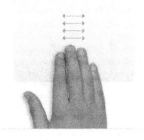

**Mission Control**
Swipe up with four fingers[3] to open Mission Control.

**App Exposé**
Swipe down with four fingers[3] to see all windows of the app you're using.

**Swipe between full-screen apps**
Swipe left or right with four fingers[3] to move between desktops and full-screen apps.

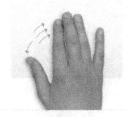

**Look up and data detectors**
Tap with three fingers to look up a word or take actions with dates, addresses, phone numbers, and other data.

**Show desktop**
Spread your thumb and three fingers apart to show your desktop.

**Launchpad**
Pinch your thumb and three fingers together to display Launchpad.

**Swipe between pages**
Swipe left or right with two fingers to show the previous or next page.

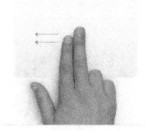

**Open Notification Center**
Swipe left from the right edge with two fingers to show Notification Center.

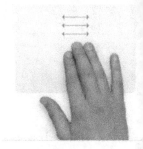

**Three finger drag**
Use three fingers to drag item on your screen, then click or tap to drop. Turn on this feature in Accessibility preferences[2].

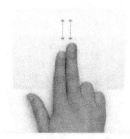

**Scroll**
Slide two fingers up or down to scroll.[1]

**Zoom in or out**
Pinch with two fingers to zoom in or out.

**Rotate**
Move two fingers around each other to rotate a photo or other item.

**Tap to click**
Tap with one finger to click.

**Secondary click (right-click)**
Click or tap with two fingers.

**Smart zoom**
Double-tap with two fingers to zoom in and back out of a webpage or PDF.

54

## Mouse gestures

For more information on these gestures, go to Apple menu, select System Preferences, then click on Mouse. There you can disable a gesture, change its type, and see which gestures work with your Mac. Mouse gestures require a Magic Mouse.

1. You can deactivate the trackpad in Accessibility preferences: click Apple menu System Preferences, then tap Accessibility. In the Mouse and Trackpad section, select Trackpad Options, and then deselect the Scrolling checkbox.

2. Accessibility preferences also contain finger swipe options: Choose Apple menu> System Preferences, then click Accessibility. on the Mouse and Trackpad area, click Trackpad Options. Choose Enable Drag, then choose one of the Drag Lock options from the pop-up menu. Choose the question mark icon to know more about each option.

3. In some versions, the gesture uses three fingers instead of four.

**Secondary click (right-click)**
Click the right side of the mouse.

**Scroll**
Slide one finger up or down to scroll.[1]

**Smart zoom**
Double-tap with one finger to zoom in and back out of a webpage or PDF.

**Mission Control**
Double-tap with two fingers to open Mission Control.

**Swipe between full-screen apps**
Swipe left or right with two fingers to move between desktops and full-screen apps.

**Swipe between pages**
Swipe left or right with one finger to show the previous or next page.

# CHAPTER SIXTEEN

# STEPS ON HOW TO AIRPLAY VIDEO AND MIRROR YOUR DEVICE SCREEN ON YOUR MACBOOK PRO DEVICE

You can use AirPlay to stream and share your content from your Apple devices to an AirPlay 2-compatible Apple TV or Smart TV. Stream video. Share your photos. Or the exact opposite of what appears on the screen of your device.

**Startup**

Make sure your devices meet the requirements to use AirPlay. To use Siri to play and control videos from your iOS device, add an Apple TV or AirPlay 2 compatible smart TV to the Home app and set it up in a room.

AirPlay video from an iPhone, iPad or iPod touch

Establish a connection to your iOS device to the same Wi-Fi network the same as an Apple TV or AirPlay-compatible smart TV.

Find the video you want to stream on AirPlay.

Tap. In some third-party applications, you may need to click a different icon first. In the Photos app, then tap.

Select an Apple TV or the Smart TV that supports AirPlay **Need help?**

To stop streaming, click on the app you are streaming, then select iPhone, iPad, or iPod touch from the list.

* Some video apps on iOS may not support AirPlay. If you can't use AirPlay with a video app, check the tvOS App Store to see if that app is available on Apple TV.

If the video is automatically streamed to the AirPlay device

AirPlay video can be automatically played on your iOS device on the Apple TV or AirPlay 2 compatible smart TV that you use frequently. If you open a video app and it appears in the upper left corner, the AirPlay device is already selected.

To use AirPlay with a different device, touch, then touch another device, or touch "iPhone" to stop streaming with AirPlay.

AirPlay the video from your Mac

Connect your Mac to the same Wi-Fi network as an Apple TV or AirPlay 2 compatible smart TV.

On your Mac, open the application or website you want to stream the video from.

In the video playback controls, tap.

Select Apple TV or Smart TV. need help?

To stop streaming your video, select the video playback controls and then select Turn off AirPlay.

View your iPhone, iPad, or iPod touch

Use Screen Mirroring to view the full screen of your iOS device on an AirPlay 2 compatible Apple TV or smart TV.

Connect your iOS device to the same Wi-Fi network as an AirPlay 2 compatible Apple TV or smart TV.

**Touch Screen mirroring.**

Select an Apple TV or AirPlay 2 compatible smart TV from the list. need help?

When the AirPlay passcode show on the TV screen, input the passcode on your iOS device immediately.

Your TV uses the screen orientation and aspect ratio of the iOS device. To cover your TV screen with a mirrored iOS device screen, you can change the aspect ratio or zoom setting option.

**Mirror or extend your Mac screen**

On your Mac, tap on the menu bar at the top of the screen, look for the Apple menu If you cannot see it, click on System Preferences you will select the Displays, then click on Show the mirroring options in the menu bar where available.

If the AirPlay passcode appears on the TV screen, enter the passcode on your Mac.

Change settings or stop mirroring

To change the size of the desktop mirrored on the TV, click on the menu bar. Then select the Built-in Mirror to match the size of your desktop or Mirror Apple TV to match the size of your TV.

AirPlay also allows you to use the TV as a separate screen for your Mac. Just click on the menu bar, then select Use as a separate screen.

**Do more with AirPlay**

Use Siri on your iPhone, iPad, or iPod touch to play movies and TV shows and control playback on an AirPlay 2-compatible Apple TV or Smart TV.

With your MAC, can also use the AirPlay to stream music online, podcasts, and even more other features to your Apple TV, HomePod, or other AirPlay-compatible speakers.

Add and manage AirPlay 2 compatible smartphones and TVs in the Home app.

# CHAPTER SEVENTEEN

## HOW TO PICK UP WHERE YOU LEFT OFF WITH HANDOFF ON MACBOOK PRO DEVICE

While using Handoff, you can start playing something on one device and then charge it on another without losing focus on what you're doing. For instance, when looking at a web page on your iPhone, then pick up where you left off in Safari on your Mac. You can also use Handoff with other Apple applications, like Calendar, Contacts, Pages, or Safari. Some third-party applications may also work with Handoff.

IPad app transfer icon on the left side of the dock.

To use Handoff, your devices must meet the continuity system requirements. Wi-Fi, Bluetooth, and Handoff must be turned on in System Preferences (on your Mac) and Settings (on iOS and iPadOS devices). You must sign in with the same Apple ID on all your devices.

**Tip:** When you turn on Handoff, you can use the Universal Clipboard to copy and paste text, pictures, images, and videos across all your devices.

## Enable or Disable Handoff

**Note**: If you don't see Handoff on your device, it doesn't work for Handoff.

On your Mac: tap on the Apple menu, choose System Preferences, select General, finally select Allow transfer between this Mac and your iCloud (under "Recent Items"). To turn off, you can uncheck the option box.

On iPad, iPhone, or iPod touch: go to Settings> General> Handoff, then tap to turn Handoff on. To turn it off, tap on the option box.

## Delivery between devices

From a Mac to an iOS or iPadOS device: The Handoff icon for the app you use on your Mac appears on your iPhone (below the app switcher) or iPad or iPod touch (at the bottom of the Dock). Click to continue working on the application.

.

You can also press Command-Tab to quickly switch to the application that contains the Handoff icon.